THIS LAND CALLED AMERICA: **KENTUCKY**

WITHDRAWN

CREATIVE EDUCATION

Published by Creative Education
P.O. Box 227, Mankato, Minnesota 56002
Creative Education is an imprint of The Creative Company
www.thecreativecompany.us

Book and cover design by Blue Design (www.bluedes.com)
Art direction by Rita Marshall
Printed in the United States of America

Photographs by Associated Press (The State Journal, Amy Wallot),
Corbis (Bettmann, Walter Bibikow, Raymond Gehman, David Muench),
Getty Images (Matthew Brady/George Eastman House, Richard S.
Durrance, Melissa Farlow, Jerry Gay, George Eastman House, JEFF
HAYNES/AFP, Hulton Archive, Andy Lyons, Will & Deni McIntyre,
Michael Ochs Archives, Logan Mock-Bunting, MPI, Panoramic Images,
Stock Montage, Tom Tietz)

Library of Congress Cataloging-in-Publication Data
Labairon, Cassandra.
Kentucky / by Cassandra Labairon.
p. cm. — (This land called America)
Includes bibliographical references and index.
ISBN 978-1-58341-642-6
1. Kentucky—Juvenile literature. I. Title. II Series.
F451.3.L33 2008
976.9—dc22   2007015011

First Edition
9 8 7 6 5 4 3 2 1

This Land Called America

KENTUCKY

Cassandra Labairon

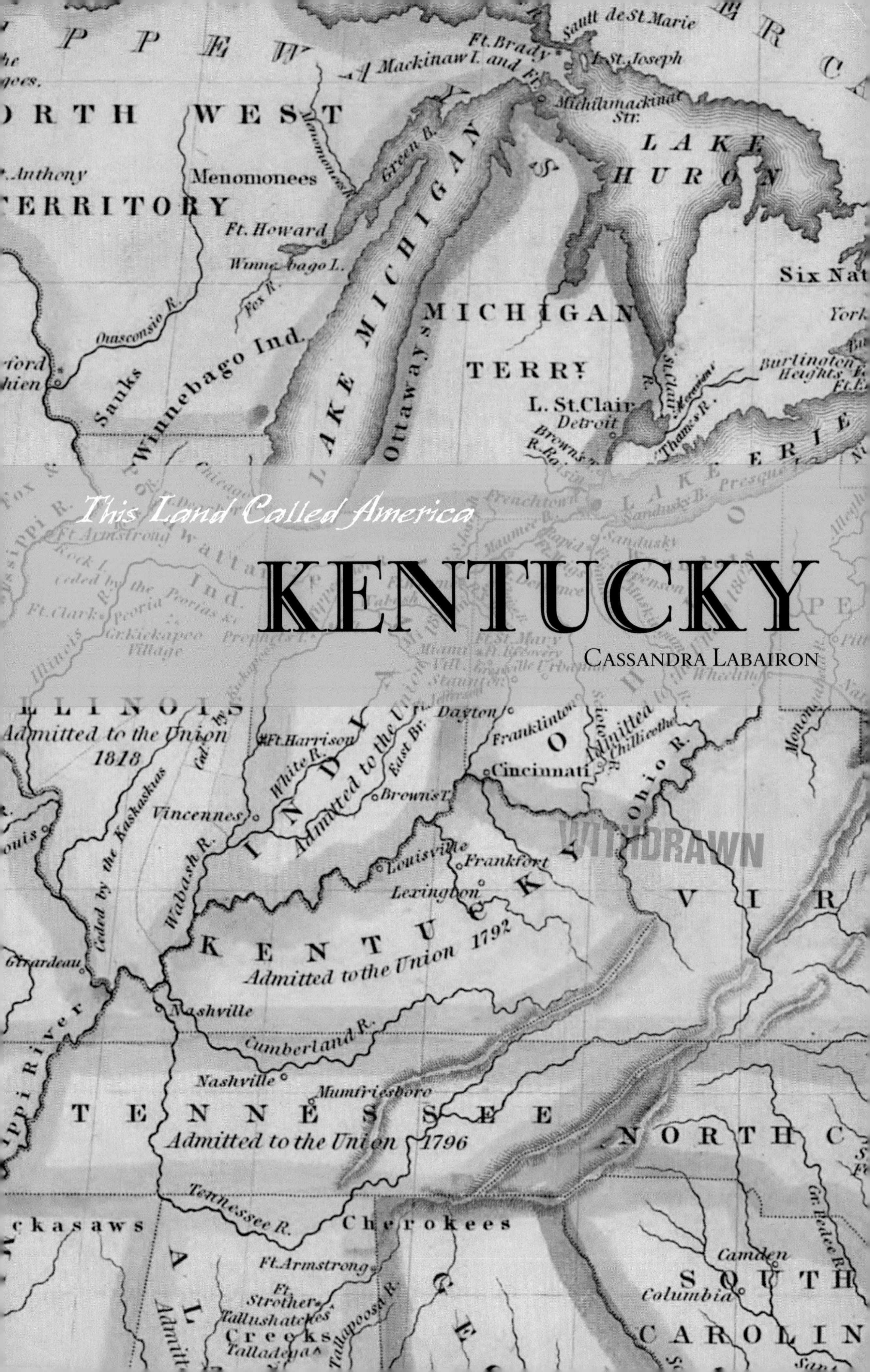

Kentucky

CASSANDRA LABAIRON

EVERY YEAR ON THE FIRST SATURDAY IN MAY, 150,000 SPECTATORS FILL LOUISVILLE'S CHURCHILL DOWNS RACETRACK TO WATCH THE KENTUCKY DERBY HORSE RACE. THE WARM SPRING AIR IS THICK WITH ANTICIPATION. FANS CHEER FOR THEIR FAVORITE HORSE AND JOCKEY. MILLIONS MORE FANS WATCH THE KENTUCKY TRADITION ON TELEVISION. AS THE ANNOUNCER EXCLAIMS, "AND THEY'RE OFF," THE HORSES BREAK INTO A GALLOP. TWO MINUTES AND A LITTLE MORE THAN ONE MILE (1.6 KM) LATER, THE WINNER CROSSES THE FINISH LINE AND IS SHOWERED WITH ROSES. SOME CALL THE RACE THE MOST EXCITING TWO MINUTES IN SPORTS, BUT A DAY AT KENTUCKY'S CHURCHILL DOWNS IS ONLY THE BEGINNING OF THE EXCITEMENT THE BLUEGRASS STATE HAS TO OFFER.

YEAR
1607 | The English colony of Virginia, which includes Kentucky, is officially established.
EVENT

North and South

As recently as 400 years ago, Kentucky's hillsides were covered in dense forests. Majestic poplar trees grew to be hundreds of years old and were as tall as 10-story buildings. Herds of buffalo grazed Kentucky's grassy valleys. Deer and turkey were plentiful, and a number of American Indian tribes used the area for hunting. The Shawnee,

Cherokee, and Delaware were three of the tribes that enjoyed Kentucky's rich hunting grounds.

Kentucky was claimed as part of the original Virginia colony when the English arrived in America in 1584. In 1750, Thomas Walker, a Virginia doctor, led an expedition into Kentucky. He was responsible for naming such landscape features as the Cumberland Gap. Walker also built the future state's first non-Indian house and was the first to find and use coal in Kentucky.

One of Kentucky's most famous early residents, Daniel Boone, followed in Walker's footsteps through the Appala-

Before horse barns (opposite) dotted Kentucky's countryside, American Indians (above) made their homes in the state's forests and valleys.

YEAR

1767–69   Wilderness explorer Daniel Boone and hunter John Finley journey into Kentucky.

EVENT

- 7 -

Daniel Boone was captured by Indians in 1778 but escaped to defend Boonesborough against further attack.

chian Mountains' Cumberland Gap in 1769. When he arrived on the other side, he found an abundance of animals such as deer and turkey and fertile land. Several years later, he and a group of farmers built a fort called Boonesborough along the Kentucky River.

After the American Revolution ended in 1783, thousands of settlers moved to Kentucky. Many people came from all of the original 13 colonies. Because the area was heavily wooded, the new settlers had plenty of materials with which to build log cabins. Communities grew quickly. The land was so beautiful and rich with vegetation and wildlife that the new settlers called it the "Eden of the West." By 1792, enough people had moved to Kentucky that it joined the United States as the 15th state.

People from Kentucky fought on both sides during the Civil War of 1861–1865. Some of Kentucky's citizens sided with the North, which wanted to end slavery. Others sided with the South, which supported slavery. Slavery was legal in Kentucky, but many white people living in the state did not like it. About 86,000 troops fought for the North, while 40,000 fought for the South. The North was victorious.

From the state's early days, Kentucky horse breeders had been breeding thoroughbred horses. After the war, horse

YEAR
1782 One of the last battles of the American Revolution is fought at Blue Licks, near Mount Olivet.
EVENT

racing became hugely popular. In 1875, Churchill Downs racetrack opened in Louisville. Soon, Kentucky became America's center for horse breeding and racing.

At the turn of the 20th century, more Americans started smoking. This increased the demand for Kentucky's tobacco crop. The growing and modernizing country needed coal from Kentucky's mines, too. Coal was used to heat homes. It was also used to power trains.

The 10 to 20 wide leaves of a tobacco plant are the parts used to make products such as cigars.

In the early part of the 1900s, conflicts arose between the hardworking people of Kentucky and the companies that profited from them. In 1904, tobacco farmers decided not to sell their crop to the American Tobacco Company because the prices were too low. Their protests allowed future farmers to have a stronger say in how they were treated, too.

Kentucky coal miners in the early 1900s also suffered. They worked in dangerous environments for usually 12 hours a day, and their wages were very low. They formed unions to help them fight for worker rights. Improvements were made, but the struggle for safe working conditions would continue for many years.

YEAR
1792 Kentucky becomes America's 15th state on June 1.
EVENT

Cumberland Gap

Kentucky's landscape is breathtaking and varied. Its 40,409 square miles (104,659 sq km) include mountains, rivers, valleys, grasslands, and meadows. Kentucky is bordered by seven states. West Virginia and Virginia are to the east. Missouri is on the western side of the state.

Parts of Illinois, Indiana, and Ohio form Kentucky's northern border, while Tennessee is immediately to the south.

Kentucky has a complex system of rivers. Three sides of the state are bordered by either the Mississippi, Ohio, Big Sander, or Tug Fork rivers. The Green River is the longest river in the state. Other rivers include the Licking, Cumberland, Kentucky, and Rolling Fork.

Most of the lakes in Kentucky are small. While some are natural, others are man-made. They were formed by the damming of rivers. The state's largest lake is Lake Cumberland. It has 1,255 miles (2,020 km) of shoreline.

The forested Cumberland Mountains (opposite) offer a contrast to the flat horse pastures (above) found in other places in Kentucky.

The Bluegrass Region and the Mississippi Plateau are in the center of the state. Most of Kentucky's racehorses are raised in the Bluegrass Region. Rich farmland is found on the higher ground of the Mississippi Plateau.

To the southeast of the Plateau are the Cumberland Mountains. The highest point in the state, Big Black Mountain, is found in this mountain range. Big Black Mountain rises 4,145 feet (1,263 m) above sea level. More mountains can be found in western Kentucky's Appalachian Plateau. This is where most of the state's coal is mined. Oil and natural gas are also found in the hills there.

YEAR
1809   Future president Abraham Lincoln is born in a log cabin near Hodgenville.
EVENT

- 13 -

The Cumberland Gap in southern Kentucky is a large break in the Appalachian Mountains. Herds of animals such as buffalo once traveled back and forth through this gap, as did the native people of the area. When settlers came, they used the Cumberland Gap to get to the other side of the mountains as well.

Today, the site of the Cumberland Gap is a national park. Each year, more than one million visitors tour the park's 18,000 acres (7,284 ha). People hike on the trails in the park. They look at the beautiful mountains. They try to spot white-tailed deer, foxes, or mink that live in the woods.

Near Lexington, about 130 miles (209 km) north of the Cumberland Gap (above), is a 600-acre (243 ha) thoroughbred horse farm (opposite) with fenced-in pastures.

1861   Kentucky declares its neutrality in the American Civil War and sends troops to fight for both sides.

Caves such as
Kentucky's Mammoth
Cave (below) are
usually found under
hilly or mountainous
ground, but some
are beneath flatter
farmland (opposite).

Mammoth Cave

Kentucky has many state and national parks. Mammoth Cave Park is a national park in the center of the state. The park contains magnificent caves, tunnels, and caverns that are part of the longest cave system in the world. More than 330 miles (531 km) of caves have been explored, and amazing formations have been discovered. However, only 12 miles (19 km) of the cave are open to visitors.

At Cumberland Falls State Park, the 68-foot (21 m) waterfall makes a rare moonbow every full moon when the light of the moon hits the mist of the waterfall. Kentucky is one of the only places in the Western Hemisphere where, on a night with a full moon, people can witness such an uncommon sight.

The weather in Kentucky is moderate for most of the year. But summers can get hot and humid, with average temperatures of about 88 °F (31 °C). The summers are particularly hot for the people who live in the southern and western parts of the state. Kentucky receives a lot of rain each year. On average, Kentucky gets 47 inches (119 cm) of precipitation annually.

YEAR

1875   The first Kentucky Derby is won by Aristedes, a horse ridden by African American jockey Oliver Lewis.

EVENT

- 17 -

Pioneers and Miners

BOTH NATIVE TRIBES AND EARLY SETTLERS WERE DRAWN TO KENTUCKY BECAUSE OF ITS RICH WILDLIFE. AFTER DANIEL BOONE CROSSED THROUGH THE CUMBERLAND GAP, OTHER FRONTIERSMEN SUCH AS JAMES HARROD WANTED TO EXPLORE THE NEW LANDS OF KENTUCKY AS WELL. HARROD, WHO WAS BORN IN PENNSYLVANIA, FOUNDED KENTUCKY'S FIRST CITY IN 1774. THE SETTLEMENT WAS NAMED HARRODSBURG IN HIS HONOR.

Settlers from Great Britain, Italy, and other countries valued the area for its fertile farmland. These hardworking people wanted to create a new life in a thriving state. As the years passed, new industries developed and jobs opened up.

The Civil War directly affected Kentucky, as two of the war's key figures came from the state. Abraham Lincoln was born in a log cabin in 1809 near Hodgenville, Kentucky. Lincoln grew up to become the 16th president of the U.S. He led the country through the Civil War, and after the war, he tried to reunite the states. Because Lincoln is considered one of the U.S.'s greatest presidents, Kentucky honors his birthplace and homestead with a historical marker and state park.

Jefferson Davis was born in 1808 in Christian County. Davis became a senator, and during the Civil War, he was elected

About 35 years after Daniel Boone blazed a trail through the Cumberland Gap (opposite), Abraham Lincoln was born in a log cabin (above).

THE RIGHT MAN, IN THE RIGHT PLACE.

JEFF. DAVIS.

OUR FIRST PRESIDENT.

president of the Confederate States of America. His armies were defeated by Lincoln and the North. After the war, Davis served two years in prison for treason. Still, he was viewed as a hero by many in the South. Today, many sculptures and monuments to Davis can be found throughout the South.

When the American Industrial Revolution began in the 1800s, Kentucky was part of it. New factories, trains, and ships needed the state's natural resources, including coal and natural gas, to generate power for all the new machines. Today, Kentucky continues to be a leading producer of transportation and electronic equipment, food and chemical products, and metals.

Kentucky also has a strong tourism industry. People come for the landscape, vibrant cities, and for the Kentucky Derby. The Kentucky Derby is the most famous horse race in America. Since 1875, the race has taken place every year at Louisville's Churchill Downs on the first Saturday in May.

Today, more than half of the people who live in Kentucky

YEAR

1892 Farmer Nathan B. Stubblefield invents an early version of the radio in Murray.

EVENT

Tobacco farmers band together in the "Black Patch Wars" against big tobacco companies.

Tobacco farmers continue to use traditional methods of curing their tobacco leaves by hanging them to dry.

Tobacco drying

live in the "golden triangle." The golden triangle is an area of the state that lies between the cities of Newport, Lexington, and Louisville. People move to the golden triangle because there are more jobs in these large cities.

Most people in Kentucky used to live on farms, and although that has changed, Kentucky farmers continue to provide valuable resources. Some tobacco farms are being converted into organic vegetable farms. Organic farms don't use man-made fertilizers or harmful chemicals to get rid of bugs. Instead, they rely on traditional crop rotation and natural fertilizers. These changes are revitalizing the farming industry and helping the environment.

YEAR

1944 The Kentucky Dam on the Tennessee River is completed, creating Kentucky Lake.

EVENT

In 2006, writer Wendell Berry was named "Kentuckian of the Year" for his efforts to bring attention to environmental issues in eastern Kentucky. Berry was born in 1934 in Henry County, Kentucky. He has written important novels, short stories, poems, essays, and nonfiction books. He values the land, and some of his books address organic farming and environmental issues.

Contemporary author Wendell Berry (above) and mid-20th-century bluegrass musician Bill Monroe (opposite) have influenced the arts in Kentucky.

1948   The University of Kentucky desegregates and begins accepting both black and white students.

Bluegrass Traditions

KENTUCKY HAS A RICH MUSICAL HISTORY. A LOT OF FOLK AND COUNTRY MUSIC WAS CREATED IN KENTUCKY. BLUEGRASS MUSIC IS A STYLE OF COUNTRY MUSIC. PEOPLE IN KENTUCKY STARTED BLUEGRASS MUSIC IN THE 1940S. THE NAME CAME FROM A BAND CALLED THE BLUE GRASS BOYS. BILL MONROE WAS THE LEADER OF THE BAND. HE IS KNOWN AS THE "FATHER OF BLUEGRASS."

Bluegrass musicians play string instruments such as mandolins, fiddles, guitars, banjos, and upright basses. The music is a blend of traditional Irish, Scottish, and African melodies and rhythms. This lively music has elements of folk, jazz, ragtime, and blues. Bluegrass is still popular today, and many people attend the state's bluegrass festivals. A few of the festivals include the Poppy Mountain Bluegrass Festival in Morehead, Aurora's Kentucky Lake Bluegrass Festival, and the River of Music Party in Owensboro.

Kentucky also has a rich tradition of folk art and crafts. The Kentucky Museum of Art and Craft in Louisville and the Kentucky Folk Art Center in Morehead are two places where visitors can learn about arts and crafts. Art lovers can find working artists and craftspeople in both the Kentucky hills and in the cities.

At the Schmidt Museum of Coca-Cola Memorabilia in Elizabethtown, visitors learn everything they ever wanted to know about Coca-Cola. If a visitor is more interested in cars

The traditions of playing bluegrass music (opposite) and eating Colonel Sanders' (above) Kentucky fried chicken continue today.

In its 2006–2007 season, the Kentucky Wildcats basketball team won 22 of its 34 games.

than Coke, he or she can visit the National Corvette Museum in Bowling Green. There, people can view models of one of America's favorite sports cars. And in Corbin, visitors can eat at the Harland Sanders Café and Museum, the original Kentucky Fried Chicken restaurant started by Colonel Sanders in the late 1930s.

Kentucky residents have a lot of state pride, which shows in their love of sports. Kentucky does not have any professional teams, but the state's colleges keep fans busy. The University of Kentucky's Wildcats have one of America's richest and most successful basketball traditions. The sports programs of the Kentucky Wesleyan Panthers, Western Kentucky Hilltoppers, and Murray State Racers entertain fans as well.

Kentucky residents have done good things for the world. A blind man named Morrison Heady helped establish the

Boxer Cassius Marcellus Clay Jr. became famous as Muhammad Ali when he changed his name in 1964.

YEAR

1966   Kentucky becomes the first Southern state to pass civil rights laws prohibiting discrimination.

EVENT

The Kentucky supreme court rules that the state school system is unconstitutional, leading to sweeping reform.

QUICK FACTS

Population: 4,206,074

Largest city: Louisville (pop. 248,762)

Capital: Frankfort

Entered the union: June 1, 1792

Nickname: Bluegrass State

State flower: goldenrod

State bird: cardinal

Size: 40,409 sq mi (104,659 sq km)—37th-biggest in U.S.

Major industries: mining, farming, manufacturing

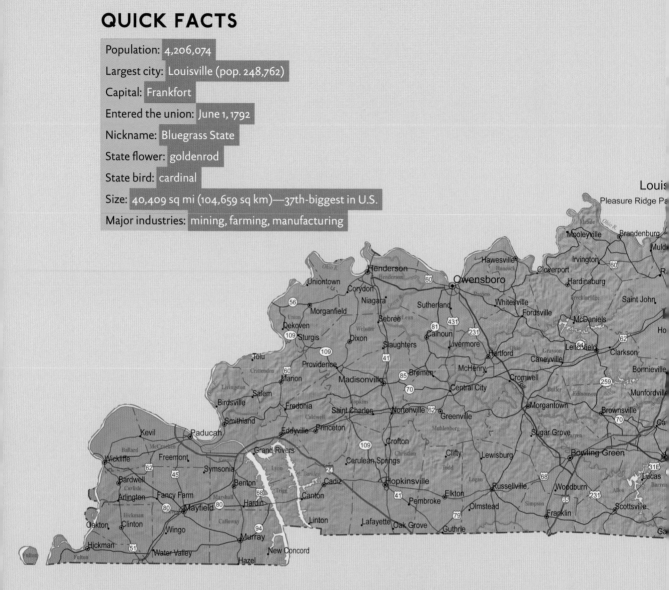

American Printing House for the Blind (APH) in Louisville in 1858. After the Civil War ended, the company started printing books in Boston Line Type, a raised-letter font similar to Braille. It was the first U.S. company to do so, and the first book the APH printed was a collection entitled *Fables and Tales for Children*.

One of the world's greatest athletes was born in Kentucky. World heavyweight boxing champion Muhammad Ali was born in Louisville in 1942. He is still known worldwide as a great fighter and humanitarian. After his retirement from

boxing in 1981, Ali wanted to make a positive difference in the
world. He began traveling to promote understanding between
people and to help feed those who were starving. His fame
brought attention to important causes.

The name Kentucky comes from an American Indian
word that means "land of tomorrow." Kentucky's rolling hills,
majestic mountains, and breathtaking forests captivate those
who see the state. Along with the landscape, the state's rich
history inspires today's Kentuckians to keep an eye on the
future, ever moving their state into tomorrow.

YEAR

2006   Author Wendell Berry is named "Kentuckian of the Year" for his environmental efforts.

EVENT

BIBLIOGRAPHY

Ciovacco, Justine, Kathleen A. Feeley, and Kristen Behrens. *State-by-State Atlas*. New York: DK Publishing, 2003.

Gutman, Bill. *The Look-It-Up Book of the 50 States*. New York: Random House, 2002.

King, David C. *Children's Encyclopedia of American History*. New York: DK Publishing, 2003.

Mead, Robin, Polly Mead, and Andrew Gutelle. *Our National Parks*. New York: Smithmark, 1992.

National Park Service, U.S. Department of the Interior. "Mammoth Cave National Park." Experience Your America. http://www.nps.gov/maca.

Young, Donald, and Cynthia Overbeck Bix. *Our National Parks*. San Francisco: Sierra Club Books, 1990.

INDEX